Walk Frankfurt

A Guide to a Short Break in Frankfurt am Main

Anne Noble

ACKNOWLEDGMENTS

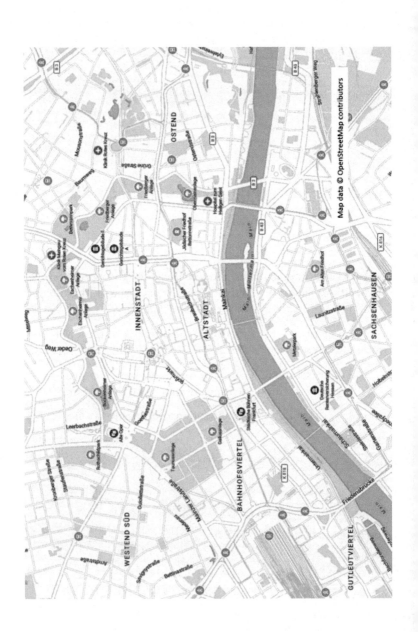

Map data © OpenStreetMap contributors

Table of Contents

Introduction

Frankfurt is a fun city. Honestly! It's small, compact, easy to navigate and perfect for an overnight stopover, weekend or longer. In the shadow of the skyscrapers lies a historic old town, an amazing array of museums, streets lined with cafes and wine bars, and markets to while away a weekend.

The River Main (*pronounced "mine"*) offers river cruises, walks along its banks and boats moored up in the summer months offering yet more refreshment. On the south side of the river lies Sachsenhausen with its apple wine taverns where young and old sit cheek by jowl on long tables and benches, tucking into large plates of hearty German fare downed with jugfuls (*bembels*) of apple wine.

The summers are warm and the festivals are plentiful. I guarantee you, there is lots to see and do in Frankfurt and following one of the walking tours in this book will give you an instant orientation and feel for the diversity Frankfurt has to offer.

This book will guide you to all the essential sights of Frankfurt and is the perfect accompaniment to a short break in the city.

Arriving in Frankfurt

By airplane

Frankfurt airport (FRA) is only 20 minutes away by local S-Bahn train from Frankfurt city centre. Trains run every 15 minutes during the day and frequently overnight.

The airport station for local trains into Frankfurt city is downstairs in Terminal 1 under Hall B. Once downstairs, the first thing to do is buy a ticket from one of the ticket machines. There are two banks of ticket machines - <u>make sure you use a green machine for local tickets</u> and not the red machines. You then have several choices of ticket:

- single journey tickets.
- a day travel card, which is cheaper than buying a return ticket, and permits travel on all the city transport for the whole day.
- a group travel card which permits up to 5 people to travel together on all the city transport for the whole day, and is excellent value if there are two or more of you.

You will need cash, or a credit/debit card with a PIN to purchase tickets from the ticket machines.

S-Bahn trains, S8 and S9, run every 15 minutes from Platform 1 and travel directly to <u>Hauptwache</u> and <u>Konstablerwache</u>, the two most central stations in Frankfurt.

> **Top Tip!** Do not confuse Frankfurt Hauptbahnhof, the main station for connecting trains, with Hauptwache in the city centre.

Frankfurt has a barrier-free transport system so you just show your ticket to the conductor during your journey.

If you need to get to an alternative city location, you can look up stations, tram-stops and ticket options using the local RMV travel service www.rmv.de.

By train

The main station in Frankfurt, Hauptbahnhof (Hbf), served with direct connections from numerous German cities as well as cities across Europe, lies approximately one kilometre west of the old town. Unfortunately the area immediately around the station is the red light district. If alighting at this station, visitors should keep their possessions safe and follow Kaiserstraße or Münchener Straße into the city centre. On a sunny day, walking along the bank of the River Main into the heart of Frankfurt is also a pleasant option. For those of you who prefer to take public transport, there are plenty of options:

- S-Bahn: the platforms are on the lower level of the main station. All city bound trains stop at Hauptwache and Konstablerwache in the city centre.
- Trams: The tram numbers 11 and 14 run to Römer/Paulskirche in the heart of the Old Town. The tram stop can be found directly outside the main exit from the main station.
- U-Bahn: the U4 and the U5 underground trains run to Dom/Römer close to the cathedral in the Old Town. Platforms for the underground are on the lower level of the main station.

Orientation

Public transport

Frankfurt has a very extensive public transport system of local trains (S-Bahn), trams (Straßenbahn), an underground (U-Bahn) and buses. The public transport provider, RMV, has a website with local area transport maps and a route finder, www.rmv.de.

To use public transport, tickets must be bought in advance from vending machines, most of which are touch-screen, where the language can be changed to English by selecting the appropriate flag logo. For bus journeys it is also possible to purchase tickets from bus drivers.

The cheapest adult ticket is the short trip, *Kurzstrecke,* ticket for journeys of less than two kilometres. For most journeys however, a single ticket, *Einzelfahrt*, is necessary. If you intend to make two or more journeys in a single day then a travel card is good value and allows you to travel on all transport modes for the day. Two types are available:

- a day travel card, *Tageskarte*, which is cheaper than buying a return ticket, and permits travel on all the city transport for the whole day.
- a group travel card, *Gruppentageskarte*, which permits up to five people to travel together on all the city transport for the whole day, and is excellent value if there are two or more of you. For group tickets the passenger names will need to be written on the ticket and proof of identity carried for inspection on the train.

You will need cash, or a credit/debit card with a PIN to purchase tickets from the ticket machines.

Cycling

Frankfurt is a very cycle friendly city with lots of cycle lanes and bike racks throughout the city. The two most popular bicycle rental services in the city are Call-A-Bike www.callabike.de and Next Bike www.nextbike.de both with English website options.

E-Scooters

E-Scooters are available to hire across Frankfurt. Bird, Bolt, Lime, Tier and Voi all have a presence in Frankfurt.

Top Tip! Lime scooters can be hired through the Uber app.

Taxis and Uber

Taxi ranks are dotted around the city and taxis can also be hailed. Licensed taxis have a lit up TAXI sign when they are available. Uber also operate in Frankfurt.

Frankfurt city centre

Frankfurt has a population of just over 750,000. It is small and compact and the heart of Frankfurt is easy to find. Just look at a map and you will notice a ring of green, the Wallanlage park, which surrounds the city centre. Within this ring of green you will find the main shopping streets, the key sights and the old town.

The old town is close to the river, its main square is known as the Römerberg. Here you will find the town hall known as the Römer, the Historische Museum, and walking in the direction of the cathedral is the area called the New Old Town, a recent development of 35 new buildings and a city planner's dream. (City planners will also appreciate the "to-scale" model of Frankfurt, see section, *The Old Jewish Cemetery and City Model*, toward the back of this book.)

Head north out of the old town and you will be in the main shopping areas of Frankfurt, ultimately reaching the Zeil, a pedestrianised street with all the usual large high street stores.

If you are interested in exploring the neighbourhoods where the locals hang out, the areas of Sachsenhausen and the Brückenviertel are just south of the river. Due north is the area known as Nordend, which has a growing reputation for great bars, restaurants and cafes.

Detailed reconstruction in the New Old Town

A potted history of Frankfurt

To understand a city like Frankfurt, which is small in size but has major economic drivers such as banking, world leading trade fairs and Germany's largest airport, it helps to know a little of its history.

Located on the River Main, Frankfurt was settled by Celts in the years BC and then by the Romans. Frankfurt came to prominence under Charlemagne, who was a Frankish king and the first Holy Roman Emperor.

Roman ruins on display in the New Old Town

It was Charlemagne who first documented the name Frankfurt in 794AD. Proclaimed as an imperial city, Emperors were both elected and crowned in Frankfurt's cathedral, and under the patronage of the Emperors, the wealth and importance of Frankfurt steadily grew throughout the middle ages.

A major source of wealth was trade fairs, with the River Main bringing in merchants from all over Europe. It was due to the trade fairs that Frankfurt developed its banking credentials, with the first bank opening in 1585.

Napoleon's arrival in 1806 did little to dampen the eminence of Frankfurt and by the mid 1800's, during calls for a united, democratic Germany, a preliminary parliament was hosted in

Frankfurt's St. Paul's church. Unfortunately the Imperial Constitution proposed by the national assembly at St. Paul's in 1849 failed to unite the German speaking lands.

It wasn't until 1871 that Germany finally united under Prussian leadership and as a result Berlin became its capital city. From this point on, through to the 1940's, Frankfurt was slowly stripped of its economic assets. The banking gravitated to Berlin and the trade fairs to Leipzig and other prominent German cities and after a 1000 years of successful commerce Frankfurt entered a decline.

Frankfurt's medieval old town, the most expansive in Germany, was all but destroyed on the night of March 22nd 1944 during a bombing raid removing many of the city's buildings and visual reminders of its historic status.

Following WW2 (World War Two) Frankfurt literally rose from the ashes and regained some of its old assets, such as banking and trade fairs, and in addition added Germany's biggest airport to its economic growth. But with Bonn elected as the new capital of West Germany, Frankfurt never quite regained the status and importance it had held during previous centuries.

The Frankfurt you experience today is a wealthy city, with a relatively small population of just over 750,000. Its architecture is a mix of post war modernist buildings with soaring skyscrapers and a scattering of beautiful, old original buildings dotted in between. In 2018 Frankfurt unveiled the "New Old Town", a city planning masterpiece of 35 new buildings, running between the cathedral and Römerberg. This project has breathed new life into the city and added yet another economic money-maker, tourism, to the city accounts, as people from all over Germany come to cast an eye over this daring recreation of what stood here before WW2.

Jewish History

Frankfurt has a Jewish history dating back to at least the 12th century. The relationship between the Jewish communities and the city are embedded in Frankfurt's trading roots. There are two excellent museums in which to discover more about Jewish life in

Frankfurt.

The **Judengasse Museum**, Battonnstraße 47, with excavated foundations of the medieval Jewish alley, *Judengasse*, focuses on day to day life and is located next door to the old Jewish cemetery and memorial to the holocaust victims.

The **Jewish Museum**, Bertha-Pappenheim-Platz 1, centres on the cultural and economic contributions by Jewish families in shaping Frankfurt as an urban metropolis.

More information about the old Jewish cemetery can be found toward the back of this book under the title, *The Old Jewish Cemetery and City Model*, and an additional Jewish memorial is mentioned in the section, East to the European Central Bank (ECB).

St Paul's - The Cradle of German Democracy

Where to stay

Frankfurt hotels are concentrated in three key areas and cater to a variety of budgets. First, the Innenstadt and old town, (outlined in blue on the map) which is the heart of the city. Second, the Bahnhofsviertal by the main railway station, the Hauptbahnhof, (outlined in red on the map) and lastly, Sachsenhausen (outlined in green on the map) famed for its apple wine taverns and lively nightlife.

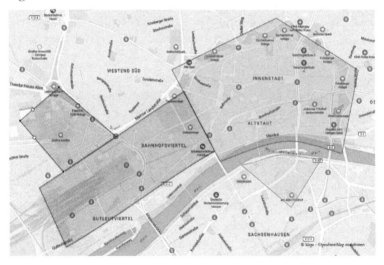

The Innenstadt and Old Town

This is the area to choose if you like to step out of your hotel and be in the heart of the city. The area is geographically identified by a green park that encircles the city centre (the park, known as the Wallanlage, is the path of the old medieval city walls). There are plenty of bars and restaurants in the heart of the city and all are accessible without the need for transportation. Walking to the river bank will take a maximum of 10 minutes and from there you have access to the south side of Frankfurt, Sachsenhausen, with its museums and apple wine taverns. If, at the end of the night, you are too tired to walk, a taxi is going to cost less than 15€ to get you back to your hotel. There is one area to be avoided in this part of the city and that is the eastern end of the Zeil, where the Zeil meets Breite Gasse. This very small, contained area is seedy and run down so worth avoiding.

More and more hotels are opening up in the city centre. Listed below are some of the most recent additions.

Hotel Motel One Frankfurt Römer
Berliner Strasse 55, Innenstadt (www.motel-one.com).
A German chain of hotels with several options in Frankfurt. Choose the Frankfurt -Römer location for easy access to the old town. Very reasonably priced with optional breakfast.

Moxy Frankfurt City Centre
Thurn-und-Taxi-Platz 8, Innenstadt (www.marriott.de).
A modern and trendy offering from the Marriott chain. Another reasonably price option, this time in the heart of the shopping area.

Sofitel Frankfurt Opera
Opernplatz 16, Innenstadt (https://all.accor.com).
Offering luxury and an up market style, this Sofitel is located opposite the old opera house.

Ruby Louise Frankfurt
Neue Rothofstrasse 3, Innenstadt (www.ruby-hotels.com).
Surprisingly well priced for a modern and centrally located hotel in the shopping area of Frankfurt. It also has a great rooftop bar!

> **Top Tip!** If hotel prices seem excessively high it's probably because there is a trade fair in town. If possible, find another date to visit Frankfurt when prices will be more reasonable.

Frankfurt Bahnhofsviertal, Hauptbahnhof and Messe

The main railway station is one kilometre to the west of the city centre and it has the biggest concentration of hotels due to the close proximity of the Messe (the trade fair exhibition centre).

Unfortunately this area also contains the red light district. The area around the station is slowly improving with a few trendy bars and some good Thai and Chinese eateries, not to mention the excellent Turkish restaurants on Münchener Straße. The hostels in this area, catering for backpackers, are well maintained, safe and security conscious. If you are booking accommodation close to the railway station then my recommendation is to book one south of Kaiserstrasse. The added advantage of being south of the station is that you are close to the river bank, which offers a lovely walk into the old town.

Hotels very close to the Messe are also away from the problem areas. However, this area is geared towards the business traveller and doesn't have much to offer except other hotel and chain restaurants.

Old Sachsenhausen and the Brückenviertel

There are a few hotels south of the river in Sachsenhausen, including the international youth hostel which is very well located for enjoying the Sachsenhausen night life of bars, restaurants and apple wine taverns. A short walk over the Eiserner Steg, a pedestrian bridge, quickly brings you to the heart of the old town.

When to visit

Seasons

May to October is definitely the best time to visit Frankfurt. In early May the city comes alive with festivals, continuing through into October. The weather is warm and reliable which encourages the cafe culture that Frankfurt has embraced, offering plenty of ice-cream parlours, coffee shops and outdoor dining. For anyone planning a longer break in Frankfurt, it is worth checking out the outdoor swimming pools (Freibad), especially on the hot days in mid-summer when the temperature can rise to the mid 30s Celsius (95F).

Autumn is the season for wine festivals. At the end of September Frankfurt hosts a 10 day Rheingau Weinmarkt along the Freßgaß. Lots of local wine producers have stands including quite a few with the VDP designation, the Verband Deutscher Prädikats- und Qualitätsweingüter e.V., an association of German wine estates offering good quality wines.

Winter can be cold with temperatures dipping below freezing, although lower than -10C (14F) is unusual. The Christmas market is the last of the annual festivals, starting at the end of November and continuing until shortly before Christmas Eve. It provides a final blast of winter fun before the city quietens down between January and April.

Sunday and Monday

Shops are closed on Sundays! Instead of shopping, the locals head for the museums, or enjoy one the many cafes, bars and restaurants which are open throughout the weekend. An alternative is to enjoy a walk through one of the city parks, along the River Main or through the city woods (*Stadtwald*).

Monday is also a quiet day in Frankfurt. Although shops are open, many cafes and museums are closed, to compensate the staff for working all weekend. If you plan to be in Frankfurt on a Monday, double check that the venue or museum you wish to visit is actually open and make a restaurant reservation to avoid disappointment.

The Museum of Modern Art aka the MMK!

Things to do

Markets

Farmers' markets are held at the end of the week in the city centre.

On Thursdays and Saturdays the farmers' market is held at **Konstablerwache**. Among the stalls selling fruit and vegetables, you will find stalls grilling sausages, selling glasses of wine, apple wine and beer, as well as plenty of places to sit and soak up the atmosphere. A couple of stalls also sell fresh apple juice (*Süßer*) that is well worth sampling.

On Fridays a market is held in **Schiller Straße** and again, among the fruit and vegetable stalls you will find vendors selling apple wine, wine and grilled sausages. A particular highlight is the Rollanderhof wine stand directly opposite the Stock Exchange which is very popular on warm summer evenings.

> **Top Tip!** At the Rollanderhof a phenomenon known as "the Frankfurt pour" takes place. The volume of 0,2l is clearly marked on the wine glass but the servers almost always pour well beyond the line. If you find yourself at an establishment where they pour to the line, drink up and find another bar!

In addition to the farmers' markets, Frankfurt has a renowned **indoor market** (*Kleinmarkthalle*) open six days a week Monday to Saturday. Within the market there are numerous stall holders offering plates of food, glasses of wine and a place to relax and sit, especially up at the mezzanine level. A particular favourite stall is Schreiber, tucked in half way along the along the butchers row, selling the traditional Frankfurter boiled sausages simply served with a bread roll and mustard. The stall is popular, so expect to queue.

A **flea market** takes place every Saturday between 9am and 2pm, alternating its location between the Mainkai on the south side of the River Main and Lindleystraße, on the north side, close to the

Osthafen. To find out the location for a particular week, check the website: www.hfm-frankfurt.de/flohmaerkte

The Indoor Market with its Rollanderhof wine bar on the upstairs terrace

Festivals

Below are listed the main festivals which take place every year. Start dates vary each year, so check the Walk-Frankfurt monthly events web page for updates: www.walk-frankfurt.com/monthly-events-in-frankfurt

JANUARY:

- **Winter   Lights   Exhibition**   -   Palmengarten, Siesmayerstraße 61, (entrance fee payable)

FEBRUARY:

- **Karneval!** – at 11.11am the carnival parades through the city centre on a Saturday (children's parade) and Sunday (main parade). Exact date changes each year and can fall in February or March.

APRIL:

- **The Spring Dippemess** - at Festplatz am Ratsweg. Three weeks of funfair rides in this suburb of Frankfurt.

MAY:

- **Night of the Museums** in Frankfurt & Offenbach. Museums are open from 7pm until 2am, ticket purchase required.
- **The Green Sauce Festival** - Roßmarkt, Frankfurt. The open-air festival is free to enter, with stalls offering food and drink.
- **The Frankfurt Rowing Festival** - Holbein Steg. Free entrance, with bands and lots to eat and drink.
- **The Freßgass Fest** - a 10 day festival of food and drink along the Freßgass (Große Bockenheimer Straße). Free entrance.

JUNE:

- **Berger Straßenfest** – all along the Bergerstraße, between Bettmannpark and Höhenstraße. Food and drink stands. Free entrance
- **Wäldchestag** - Frankfurt City Forest, an annual funfair in the woods. (Take the number 21 tram to Am Oberforsthaus). Free entrance.

JULY:

- **Opernplatz Festival** - a festival of food and drink outside the Old Opera House (Alte Oper). Free entrance.
- **Christopher Street Day** – a parade through Frankfurt and festivities at Konstablerwache.
- **Sommerwerft Theatre Fest** – a selection of performances for two weeks along the northern banks of the River Main, between Flößerbrücke & ECB. Free entrance.

AUGUST:

- **The Main Fest** – a funfair along the north bank of the

river, in the heart of the old town. Free entrance.

- **Bernemer Kerb** – Fünffingerplätzchen, Bornheim. Wine stands and food at this local five day festival. Free entrance.
- **Frankfurt Applewine Fest** - a 10 day celebration of apple wine, taking place on Roßmarkt. Free entrance.
- **Frankfurt Bahnhofsviertalnacht** - one evening a year starting at 7pm, roads are closed and the Bahnhofsviertal streets are handed over to the people of Frankfurt.
- **Museumsuferfest** – an open-air festival along both sides of the Main River. Arts and crafts on the south side, and music parties into the night. Purchase of a Museums button, will give you free access to the museums along the Ufer all weekend.

SEPTEMBER:

- **Frankfurt Rheingauer Weinfest** - A wine festival along the Freßgass (Große Bockenheimer Straße). Free entrance.
- **The Autumn Dippemess** – at Festplatz am Ratsweg. Three weeks of funfair rides in this suburb of Frankfurt.
- **Harvest Festival** - Roßmarkt. An open-air festival showcasing local farmers and produce.

OCTOBER:

- **Federweisser Fest** - Liebfrauenberg, Frankfurt. A two week festival celebrating the freshly fermented grape juice from the recent harvest. Free entrance.
- **The German Jazz Festival** – usually at the end of October. Jazz concerts (fees payable) are hosted at various venues around the city.

NOVEMBER – DECEMBER:

- **The Christmas Market** – Römerberg, Frankfurt Old Town. Four weeks of festivities and glüwein, with art fairs being hosted in The Römer and St. Paul's church nearby.

Shopping

Most shops open at 10am, except supermarkets and department stores which open a little earlier. Closing times vary, but in the city centre it is usually 7pm. For independent retailers it is best to check their opening hours on-line.

Shopping Streets

The Zeil is one of the busiest, pedestrianised, shopping streets in Germany running from Hauptwache in the west to Konstablerwache in the east. It has all the usual brands of retailers, plus the German department stores Galleria and Karstadt. The "My Zeil" shopping mall, half way along the Zeil, has more of the usual shops and restaurants on the upper level and a supermarket in the basement.

> **Top Tip!** Galleria has a canteen style restaurant and café on its top floor with an outdoor terrace which has good views across the city.

Goethestraße is the place to head to for international designer shops and high end jewellers, such as Chanel and Cartier. Not far from the northern end of Goethestraße is Manufactum, Bockenheimer Anlage 49-50. This shop houses a collection of artisan goods and is a great place to browse, and grab some refreshment at the in-house cafe.

Oeder Weg leads north from Eschenheimer Turm and has a mix of cafes and independent stores. For some fun, colourful, locally made pottery head to Birgit Palt Pottery, Oeder Weg 50.

Berger Straße, to the east of the city centre, offers a long meander through a popular residential area, with cafes and a mix of independent retailers. At the westerly beginning of Berger Straße is the small and pretty Bethmannpark with a beautiful Chinese garden.

Fahrgasse leading down from Konstablerwache is the go-to street for art galleries and it makes for an interesting walk on your way to Sachsenhausen via the Alte Brücke.

Brückenstraße and **Wallstraße** in Sachsenhausen offer local designer boutiques and second hand record stores among the cafes and restaurants. Töpferei Maurer, Wallstraße 5 is a pottery specialising in authentic Bembels, and smaller Bembel related goods, which make great souvenirs.

Bembel-Maurer on Wallstraße in Sachsenhausen

Supermarkets

A Tegut supermarket is located near the Eschenheimer Tor on Bleichstraße 57, and close to the Hauptbahnhof on Kaiserstraße 62-64.

In the basement of the My Zeil shopping mall, Zeil 106, is a Rewe supermarket.

Food halls are in the basements of both the Galleria department stores located near Hauptwache and Konstablerwache.

Aldi has a store in the city centre on Töngesgasse 40.

Souvenirs

Souvenir shops selling the usual trinkets are plentiful around the Römerberg in the heart of the old town. For traditional German crafted goods, including Christmas and other seasonal decorations, head to Handwerkkunst, Braubachstraße 39.

Kulturothek, Markt 32, offers a better quality of souvenirs in the heart of the New Old Town.

Hessen Shop, An der Kleinmarkthalle, is another souvenir shop offering some better quality momentos.

> **Top Tip!** Museum shops are a great place to pick up a souvenir and they are open on Sundays and public holidays too.

The Städel Museum

Museums

Frankfurt has an impressive 38 museums, many of which are located along the southern bank of the River Main, the *Schaumainkai,* and in the city centre.

If you intend to visit two or more museums during your stay, then a Museumsufercard is cost effective, offering free entrance for two consecutive days to all museums. On the last Saturday of the month, many museums are also free to enter.

Be aware that many museums are <u>closed on Mondays</u>, and might be temporarily closed during a change of exhibition. Some exceptions to Monday closing are:

Naturmuseum Senckenberg
Senckenberganlage 25, Westend (<u>www.senckenberg.de</u>). A natural history museum. Great for kids as well as adults.

Palmengarten
Siesmayerstraße 63, Westend (<u>www.palmengarten.de</u>). A botanical garden with an area of 22 hectares and around 13,000 plant species.

Both the above museums are open seven days a week, as is the Carmelite Cloister (sight no. 28 during the second walking tour in this book, *Hauptwache and Beyond*)

All current information regarding opening times and exhibitions can be found at: <u>www.museumsufer.de/en</u>.

Some museums only offer exhibit information in German. A few which do have English translations are listed below.

Museum of Modern Electronic Music
An der Hauptwache, Innenstadt (<u>https://tickets.momem.org/</u>). The MOMEM is the first museum of its kind and has late opening until 9pm during the week.

Caricatura Museum
Weckmarkt 17, Innenstadt (<u>https://caricatura-museum.de/</u>). An interesting delve into German humour and satire in the form of caricature.

Historisches Museum Frankfurt
Saalhof 1, Innenstadt (<u>www.historisches-museum-frankfurt.de/</u>). An excellent museum noted for its detailed, to scale, model of Frankfurt's old town pre and post WW2.

Schirn Kunsthalle
Römerberg, Innenstadt (<u>www.schirn.de/</u>). A small art museum

which showcases visiting exhibits

Städel Museum

Schaumainkai 63, Sachsenhausen (www.staedelmuseum.de/en). A pilgrimage for any art lover.

Museum für Kommunikation

Schaumainkai   53   Sachsenhausen   (www.mfk-frankfurt.de/). Communication across the decades, from old postal carriages to modern age devices. The basement also displays the workings of an old telephone exchange.

Tourist Office and Attractions

There are some great things to see and do that are uniquely Frankfurt and the local tourist board can advise on optimal ways to maximise your time and spend whilst visiting. Tourist board offices can be found at the main station, in the Bahnhofshalle, close to the main exit and in the Old Town, directly on the Römerberg (Römerberg 27). The offices are open 7 days a week and there is also a website www.frankfurt-tourismus.de/en

Discounted Tickets

The Frankfurt card, which can be bought from the tourist office, www.frankfurt-tourismus.de/en/Information-Planning/Frankfurt-Card, is great value if you would like to use public transport and have discounted entry to many of the city attractions and museums. Frankfurt cards can be bought for durations of one or two days and be for individuals or groups of up to 5 people. The card includes travel to and from the airport, so if using it on the day of arrival, buy the Frankfurt card in advance, on-line.

River Cruise

On a sunny day a boat trip on the Main is worth doing. The Primus Line boats loop to the east and then to the west. A loop takes 50 minutes or combine the two to while away 100 minutes. Refreshments are served on board. The departure point (on the hour and half-hour) is next to the Iron Bridge, *Eiserner Steg*, in the Old Town. Tickets can be bought at the kiosk or on-line in advance, www.primus-linie.de/en

Apple Wine Express

The Ebbelwei-Express is Frankfurt's very own colourful tram, wending its way through the streets with an on-board commentary. It runs on Saturdays, Sundays and public holidays, you may alight at any one of its regular stops. Tickets can be bought on the tram and includes an apple wine or non-alcoholic beverage. It's certainly a novel way to see the city! The timetable, ticket prices and planned stops can be found on the website: www.ebbelwei-express.de/en/information/timetable-and-fares

Main Tower

If views across the city and beyond are your thing, then a trip to the top of the 200m high Main Tower, Neue Mainzer Straße 52–58, should satisfy. Tickets are best bought on the day to avoid disappointment if it's rainy or there is low cloud cover. http://www.maintower.de/en

> **Top Tip!** The Main Tower also has a restaurant and lounge bar on the 53rd floor with great views across the city. The restaurant, open from 6pm, has recently been awarded a Michelin star so early reservation is recommended. The lounge bar is open from 9pm.

Frankfurt Skyline

The Frankfurt skyline is the "must-have" photo of any trip to Frankfurt. Head to the Alte Brücke, just two hundred meters east of the Iron Bridge, to capture a good shot. For an even better shot on a clear night head further east and join the professionals lining up on the Ignatz-Bubis-Brücke.

Good to know – in Germany

Cash or Card?

Cash is still popularly used in Germany. The Covid pandemic encouraged card use and contactless payment, but in smaller shops, some restaurants and at markets, don't be surprised if cards are not accepted. It is worth keeping a few Euros on hand for those moments.

It is still possible to exchange currency at the airport, but elsewhere in Frankfurt your best option is to use an ATM. There are numerous banks around Roßmarkt, near Hauptwache; a Deutsche Bank and Sparkasse bank at Konstablerwache and post office ATMs at Goetheplatz and in the Karstadt department store on the Zeil.

Carrier Bags

Shops will charge you for a **shopping bag**, regardless of what your purchase is. Use of plastic bags is also being phased out, even at the markets, so if possible keep a carrier bag with you. Cloth bags with motifs are very popular in Germany and are a cheap keepsake if returning overseas.

Pronunciation

The ß is pronounced as "ss" hence, for us English speakers, Straße is equivalent to Strasse!

Spotting the difference in "ie" and "ei" is a tough one but has a big effect on the word. The ie is pronounced like ee as in, bee or keep. The ei is pronounced like eye, for example while or mile.

The Germans love to string words together. A great example observable throughout Frankfurt city centre is "Schritttempo" meaning walking pace, made up of Schritt = step and tempo = pace. You'll see the word on signs requesting cyclists to go slow in pedestrian areas. The word is also a fine example of three identical consonants together in one word, something the German language permits but not found in English.

Schritttempo = walking pace (or should that be walkingpace?)

Dining and Bars

It is possible to find all dining options in Frankfurt, from McDonalds to 3-star Michelin restaurants. The places listed below are a few of the local highlights. More recommendations can be found on the www.walk-frankfurt.com website, along with a blog page dedicated to gluten free, vegan and vegetarian dining options.

Breakfast

Bakeries open early in Frankfurt and are a good option for a quick bite to eat and a coffee first thing in the morning.

Kaiser Zeit
Kaiser Straße 59, Bahnhofsviertal & Börsenplatz 1, Innenstadt (www.ihre-bio-baeckerei.de).
Open from 7am weekdays and 8am at the weekend, this bakery offers organic breads, drinks and places to sit and eat.

MainKai Cafe Bistro
Mainkai 15, Innenstadt (www.mainkaicafe.de).
Open at 9am this cafe offers vegan and gluten-free options too.

Cafe Libretto
Hasengasse 4, Innenstadt (www.cafe-libretto.de).
Open at 8am weekdays, 9am on Sundays, offering a breakfast menu. Centrally located and close to the cathedral.

Bull + Bear Cafe
Schillerstrasse 11, Innenstadt (www.bullandbear.de).
Open at 8am, and 9am on Sundays. This is a reliable place for an early start in Frankfurt.

Lunch

Kleinmarkhalle
Hasengasse 5, Innenstadt (http://kleinmarkthalle.de).
The indoor market is as casual as it gets with lots of stalls offering a variety of cuisines: Indian food, vegan specialities, Italian, and of course Schreibers and its simple offering of the local Frankfurt

sausage, as mentioned in the Markets section of this book.

Heininger

Neue Krämer 31, Innenstadt (www.metzgerei-heininger.de).
Heininger offers traditional German food and canteen style service.
It keeps regular shop hours Mon-Sat, and is not open in the evening.
There is lots of seating inside as well as seating outdoors. Service is
friendly and the dishes good value.

The pretty garden at the Restaurant Klosterhof

Restaurant Klosterhof

Weißfrauenstrasse 3, Innenstadt (www.klosterhof-frankfurt.de).
If you prefer a restaurant with service the Restaurant Klosterhof,
tucked away next to the Carmelite Cloister (no. 28 on the walking
tour), serves up plates of traditional Frankfurt food. In the summer
it has a lovely outdoor seating area.

Fisch Franke

Domstraße 9-11, Innenstadt (www.fischfranke.de).
This restaurant is a Frankfurt institution serving excellent,
traditional, fish dishes. A slightly older clientele, but so what!

Dinner

Restaurant Klosterhof and **Fisch Franke**, listed in the previous lunch section, are also open into the evening. Fisch Franke closes earlier than most restaurants though, so early evening dining is recommended.

Carte Blanche
Egenolffstrasse 39, Nordend (**www.carteblanche-ffm.de**).
Wonderful, surprise menus based upon the freshest of ingredients purchased by the chef at the market that day.

Bidlabu
Kleine Bockenheimer Str 14, Innenstadt (**www.bidlabu.de**).
Small, tightly packed tables with a limited but finely executed menu. A hidden gem.

Jasper's
Schifferstr. 8, Sachsenhausen (**www.jaspers-restaurant.de**).
Tucked away in a courtyard, this restaurant oozes traditional French bistro charm.

L'Ecume
Friedberger Landstr. 62, Nordend (**www.restaurant-lecume.de**).
More expensive than the other listings with an innovative menu, spend €€'s and go for the champagne accompaniment.

Metropol am Dom
Weckmarkt 15, Innenstadt (www.metropolcafe.de/)
Offering some vegetarian and vegan options, this is a laid-back, reasonably priced café/restaurant. It has a sunny garden area and great cakes too!

Badidas
Römerberg 6a, Innenstadt next to the Schirn Art Gallery
(https://badias.de/cafe-and-restaurant).
Real Mediterranean flair and some tasty vegetarian platters in the heart of the "new" old town. Nice outdoor seating too.

Apple wine taverns

Apple wine taverns, *Apfelwein Lokal,* are a unique feature of Frankfurt, with the majority being found in Old Sachsenhausen. Seating is often first come, first served, with strangers and friends crammed together on long tables and benches. The food is good and hearty with lots of local dishes which perfectly compliment apple wine, the famed local drink of Hessen and commonly called *Äppler.*

Rather than being wine, Äppler is more like a sour cider, with an average alcohol content of 4 to 5%. Locals order it in large blue and grey jugs, called *bembels,* together with a bottle of sparkling water, which they add to the apple wine to soften down the sourness. The ribbed glass, called a *gerippte,* from which apple wine is drunk serves a practical purpose. The pattern is to stop the glass from slipping through your fingers, which is a very likely peril after a bratwurst or two.

If you are not sure what size bembel to order, allow your waiter to decide. They can usually guess accurately how much you and your friends are likely to consume!

Traditional Frankfurt dishes

The traditional Frankfurt dishes to complement your Äppler include:

Handäse mit Musik (cheese with onions) - a potent, locally made, cheese served smothered with a little vinaigrette, raw onions and bread. An ideal starter. Yes, mit Musik does translate as "with music" and it is referring to the music you will create the next day after consuming all those onions!

Frankfurter Grüne Soße (green sauce) - traditionally served with boiled potatoes and boiled egg. The green sauce is made from freshly chopped chives, cress, chervil, parsley, pimpernel, sorrel and borage mixed with a little sour cream chopped egg and seasoning.

Frankfurter Würstchen - the local, finely minced, boiled pork sausage usually served with potato salad.

Rindwurst - a boiled sausage made of beef. Often served with sauerkraut.

Frankfurter Green Sauce, simply served with boiled egg and potato

Top Tip! Instead of dessert why not try a *Mispelchen*, which consists of a medlar fruit, with apple brandy poured over. Look around, you'll notice various locals enjoying a Mispelchen or two!

A tray of Mispelchen – because one is never enough!

Popular apple wine taverns

Many of the taverns do not open until after 4pm but if they are open for lunch it has been noted below.

Lorsbacher Thal
Große Rittergasse 49, Sachsenhausen (**www.lorsbacher-thal.de**).
Open for lunch Sat & Sun. Known for their speciality apple wines, as well as the Äppler. A beautiful courtyard setting in the summer months, there is also a sister restaurant on Neue Wall 9, Sachsenhausen.

Fichtekränzi
Wallstraße. 5, Sachsenhausen (**www.fichtekraenzi.de**).
Friendly service and lots of traditional dishes. Popular with ex-pats as well locals, so the staff are used to dealing with English speakers.

Atschel
Wallstraße 7, Sachsenhausen (**www.atschel-frankfurt.de**).
Open at lunch time! A very traditional apple wine tavern popular with the locals. Often very busy and you might have to wait to be seated.

Klaane Sachsehäuser
Neue Wall 1, Sachsenhausen (**www.klaanesachsehaeuser.de**).
Plenty of cover in the courtyard, for those warm but drizzly evenings.

Zum Gemalten Haus
Schweizer Str. 67 Sachsenhausen (**www.zumgemaltenhaus.de**).
  Open at lunchtime. Of the two apple wine taverns on Schweizer Strasse, this one has a less touristy feel and friendlier service.

Zur Sonne
Bergerstraße 312, Bornheim (**https://zur-sonne-frankfurt.de**).
Open Sunday lunchtime. Take the U-Bahn U4 to Bornheim Mitte, or enjoy walking the length of Bergerstrasse (20 minutes) before arriving at Zur Sonne for dinner.

More recommendations for apple wine taverns and restaurants can be found via the Walk-Frankfurt blog (www.walk-frankfurt.com/blog)

Wine bars

Frankfurt is on the doorstep of the Rhinegau wine region and has access to some excellent local Rieslings. If you think German wine is sweet, then think again. Rheingau Rieslings are dry, *trocken*, with tingling acidity. All the wine bars listed offer good German wines as part of their selection. In addition, check the Markets section in this guide for hints of other places to sample some local wines.

Weinschirn
Römerberg 8, Innenstadt (**www.weinschirn.de**).
A good selection of German wines, and tasty snacks of cheese, hams and flammkuchen (a very thin, pizza like base, traditionally topped with onions, bacon and crème fraiche.) Find Weinschirn tucked around the back of the Römerberg, opposite the U-Bahn exit.

Balthasar Ress Weinbar
Markt 13a, Innenstadt (**www.balthasar-ress.de/weinbar-frankfurt**).
A slightly pricier wine bar than most, serving their own wines from

the Rheingau region.

Raum & Wein

Friedberger Landstraße 86, Nordend (www.raumundwein.de).
Although it looks like a wine shop, it is also a place to sit and enjoy a glass or two of wine with friends. Great wines and very popular with the locals.

Die Weinbar Sachsenhausen

Große Rittergasse 89, Old Sachsenhausen (www.die-weinbar-sachsenhausen.eatbu.com).
A good selection of wines and snacks such as olives, cheese and flammkuchen, to be found in the heart of old Sachsenhausen.

Weinschirn – good wines and friendly service!

Beer specialists

You can find the classic Frankfurt Binding beer in all the local bars, but for something a little different try the places listed here. Also, head to the Konstablerwache farmers' market on a Thursday or Saturday where there is a local craft beer stand.

Wir Komplizen
Egenolffstraße 17, Nordend, (<u>www.wir-komplizen.de</u>).
Excellent German and international craft beers, in a courtyard set back from the street. Also has a snack menu that includes vegan options.

Braustil
Oeder Weg 57, Nordend (<u>www.braustil.de</u>).
A short walk from the city centre, along this interesting street, will bring you to this small bar with a quirky beer garden in a former gas station forecourt. A lovely selection of craft beers and a BBQ smokehouse menu to compliment.

Naiv Bar & Restaurant
Fahrgasse 4, Innenstadt (<u>www.naiv-frankfurt.de</u>).
Craft beers on tap and lots of food options.

Zum Bitburger
Hochstraße 54, Innenstadt (<u>www.zumbitburger.com</u>).
Not many choices of beer, however Bitburger is a great lager and this is a very cosy bar to hang out in on cold days and evenings. It also serves traditional German food at lunch and dinner time.

> **Top Tip!** On a warm summer evening head to one of the boats moored along the south side of the River Main to enjoy a drink and absorb the atmosphere. Close to the Untermainbrücke, is the Maincafe serving drinks from within the river embankment walls (<u>https://maincafe.net</u>) and if you really want to get down with the locals walk along to the Main Cocktail Bar, close to the junction with Zum Gipfelhof, down on the river bank. (<u>www.main-cocktailbar.de</u>)

Coffee

Some of the fun in travelling is finding out how the locals like their brew. The flat white has made its way to Frankfurt so there is good variety of traditional versus trendy places to grab your fix. Starbucks is here too, for those of you looking for the taste of home and a reliable wi-fi connection.

Wacker's Kaffee

Kornmarkt 9, Innenstadt (https://wackerskaffee.de).

A traditional coffee roaster selling bags of whole beans as well as fresh cups of coffee straight from the Espresso machine. The brew is strong and slightly bitter. Cappuccinos pack a punch without an extra shot and are served cup sized (125ml). It's possible to pick up a ham or cheese roll, or pastry in the morning and some good cakes in the afternoon.

The Espresso Bar

Schäfergasse 42-44, Innenstadt
(www.facebook.com/TheEspressoBARfrankfurt/).

Barely more than a hole in the wall with place enough to stand and drink, serving seriously good espressos and cappuccinos. Proper cup sized portions, none of this over-sized, laden with milk, nonsense from these people!

Hoppenworth & Ploch Altstadt

Markt 22, Innenstadt (https://hoppenworth-ploch.de/pages/cafe-altstadt).

A decent espresso café in the heart of the old town, serving a few snacks too. It's a popular place and rightly so, with seating indoors and outdoors in the pretty market square.

One of the "bar" boats which moor along the river banks

The Holy Cross Brewing Society

Fahrgasse 7, Innenstadt

(www.facebook.com/TheHolyCrossBrewingSociety/).

More than just an espresso bar, the HCBS does a full range of coffees and is the place to go if you like pour-over and filter styles. It's popular, and the espresso here is mild and not so punchy. Small plates of food are available for breakfast & lunch and locals come here for the variety of top branded roasted beans on sale.

Walking Tour - Altstadt

The following chapters offer two walking tours and some further suggestions of what to see and visit if you have more time in Frankfurt.

The Altstadt walking tour has a duration of one hour and can be linked together with the second tour in this book *Hauptwache and Beyond.* The two walks combined will take two hours to complete.

To find the starting point for this tour, at the old town hall (Römer), take the U4/U5 train to Dom/Römer or take the tram 11 or 14 to Römer/Paulskirche. Alternatively take numerous choices of public transport to Hauptwache or Konstablerwache. It will only take 5 minutes to walk down to the old town

A highlight of the Altstadt tour is walking through the newly constructed (2018) New Old Town, *Neu Altstadt,* with its recreated 35 buildings in both contemporary and replica styles.

The Neu Altstadt project has brought back to life 7,000 m² (8,000 yd²) of the old town that was obliterated in 1944. In 2012 the city put into action this exciting new development which copied the footprint of the buildings that stood here before the war and re-opened the Coronation Way, a footpath trodden by the Holy Emperors and their processions. Also preserved are the archaeological ruins dating back to Roman (100AD) and Carolingian times (800AD), which are free to enter. When exploring this area, imagine it expanding over 28,000 m², four times the size it is today, which was the original size of Frankfurt's expansive medieval old town.

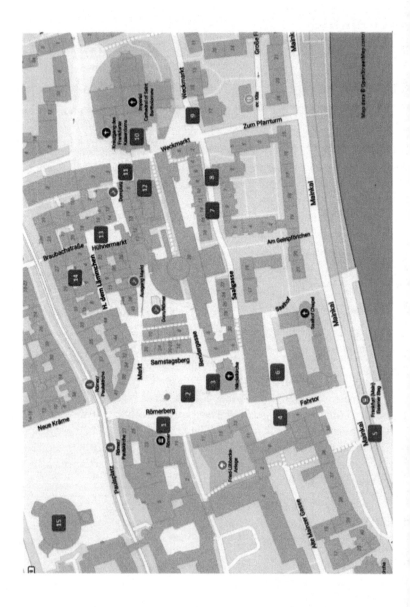

1. Römerberg

This is the heart of the old town, the place where the earliest trade fairs were held and from which the medieval city made its wealth. Known as the Römerberg, today it presents a picturesque old town square and still hosts the Frankfurt Christmas market every year.

The Town Hall, Römer

You can't fail to notice the old town hall, the *Römer*, the large pink sandstone building with flags flying over the balcony. Above the balcony are the statues of four Holy Roman Emperors, from left to right:

- Friedrich I, also known as Barbarossa, the first Holy Roman Emperor to be elected at Frankfurt in 1152;
- Ludwig the Bavarian who bestowed the Spring trade fair to Frankfurt in 1330;
- Karl IV the creator of the 1356 Golden Bull document making the Frankfurt the election city;
- Maximillian II the first emperor to be crowned at Frankfurt cathedral in 1562.

The town hall has grown over the centuries and incorporates 11 different buildings in its foundations. In 1405 the first house acquired to serve as the town hall was a house called "Zum Römer" and the name Römer has stuck to this day.

> **Top Tip!** The Kaisersaal, the ceremonial hall inside the Römer, is open to visitors (entrance fee payable) and displays portraits of all the Holy Roman Emperors. The entrance can be found along the Limpurgergasse.

Centre stage of the Römerberg is the Lady Justice fountain. She looks directly at the town hall, scales and sword in hand, and notably without a blind fold.

Opposite the town hall, on the eastern side of the square, stands a row of timber-framed houses erected in the 1980s, which are replicas of what stood here before WW2. The ornate, brown house with a turret, to the left of the row, was the first bank in Frankfurt, which opened in 1585. (Go to point 8 – Saalgasse, for an additional note about these buildings).

Timber-framed houses on the eastern side of the Römer

2. Book Burning Memorial

As you head towards the St. Nicholas church on the Römerberg, keep a look out for the large brass book burning memorial plaque nestled among the cobbles. It commemorates the site of the Student Union led book burnings on May 10th 1933, one of the earliest displays of inciting hatred against those considered to be encouraging un-German (non Nazi) ideals. In this case it included among others, authors who were left wing or political objectors, Jewish, disabled or considered immoral.

The Book Burning Memorial

3. St. Nicholas church (*Alte Nikolai*)

Römerberg 11

The protestant St. Nicholas church on the south side of the Römerberg has foundations dating back to the 12th century. Its Carillon bells ring out daily across the square at 9:05am, 12:05pm and 5:05pm.

If it is open, take a look inside the church and view the two distinctive sets of stained glass windows. The yellow hued windows behind the alter were created by Lina von Schauroth and installed in the 1950's. On the south and west wall a different set of windows display magnificent shades of red, blue and gold and, although being very different in style, they are by the same artist. These windows are from the estate of Carl von Weinberg and commissioned in the 1920's for his own chapel. However, in the 1930's, because of his Jewish heritage, the Nazi party forced the sale of von Weinberg's estate. Lina von Schauroth rescued the windows and safely stored them during von Weinberg's exile in Italy. Carl von Weinberg died in exile and today the stained glass windows are installed in the St. Nicholas church, along with Lina von Schauroth's other work.

4. House Wertheym (*Haus Wertheym*)

Fahrtor 1

House Wertheym is the only original renaissance house in Frankfurt's old town to survive the bombing campaigns of the Second World War. Its survival is due to its location along a key escape route. The night of March 22nd 1944 saw the most destructive bombing raid on Frankfurt's old town. The densely packed, timber-framed, medieval houses quickly caught fire and people fled to the river bank for safety. Keeping the path leading to the river open was a priority, so the fire-fighters concentrated their efforts on preventing Haus Wertheym from collapsing and blocking the escape route. The destruction that night was immense and 80% of the Old Town was destroyed.

> **Top Tip!** The bakery next door to Haus Wertheym, Condit Couture, has excellent cakes and good ice-cream too!

5. The Iron Bridge (*Eiserner Steg*)

Built in 1868, the Iron Bridge has great views up and down the River Main. On the north bank stand the Frankfurt skyscrapers. Seventeen of Germany's 18 skyscrapers stand in Frankfurt. The tallest building in Germany at 259m is the Commerzbank Tower, viewable from the bridge. Upstream, looking east, is the beautiful glass tower of the European Central Bank.

The area south of the river is Sachsenhausen, and the south bank is known as the Museums Row, *Museumsufer*. Included along this row are the Film Museum, the Architectural Museum and the Städel Art Museum.

6. Historical Museum of Frankfurt

Saalhof 1 (www.historisches-museum-frankfurt.de)

This lovely museum is great for history buffs. It contains an interesting to-scale model of Frankfurt's old town before and after the WW2 bombings depicting the extent of the destruction. The museum has special exhibits for children and an excellent café too.

7. Stumble Stones (*Stolpersteine*)

Saalgasse 9

Look down on the ground to see the brass stumble stones (Stolpersteine) of the von Halle family. Stumble stones are the initiative of Gunter Demnig, and they commemorate "...the victims of National Socialism, keeping alive the memory of all Jews, Roma and Sinti, homosexuals, dissidents and Jehovah's Witnesses and victims of euthanasia who were deported and exterminated." The commemorative stumble stones are placed in the ground outside the residence where the victim last freely lived with the opening words, "Here lived...", followed by a short narrative of the victim's fate. Frankfurt has 1,700 of the 61,000 stumble stones which exist across Europe.

HIER WOHNTE
KATHARINA SCHMID
JG. 1889
ZEUGIN JEHOVAS
VERHAFTET 1937
MORINGEN
RAVENSBRÜCK
1941 AUSCHWITZ
1945 BERGEN-BELSEN
TOT 22.2.1945

A stumble stone laid for Katharina Schmid

8. Saalgasse

Saalgasse 2-18

The row of tall, individually designed, houses along the Saalgasse were erected in the 1980's but this was not their intended location. They were originally designed for the Römerberg, but the people of Frankfurt turned against the modernist buildings and lobbied, instead, for the replica houses that now proudly stand opposite the town hall.

9. Caricatura Museum

Weckmarkt 17   (www.caricatura-museum.de)

A former textile warehouse dating back to 1399, today the *Leinwandhaus* houses the Caricatura Museum. The exhibits of satirical cartoons offer an insight into some great German humour.

10. Frankfurt Cathedral

Kaiserdom Domplatz 1

Frankfurt Cathedral is of catholic denomination and dedicated to

St. Batholomew. A place of worship since 680 AD, the Gothic structure you see today is from between the 13th & 15th centuries. The cathedral was a place of Holy Roman Empire elections from 1356 and coronations from 1562. If it is open, feel free to go in and take a look around.

> **Top Tip!** The bell tower, of 328 steps, is open to the public (entrance on the south side of the cathedral) for a fee and offers a great view across the rooftops of the old town.

11. Golden Scales House (*Haus zur goldener Waage*)

Markt 5

Directly opposite the cathedral, the original Golden Scales house was commissioned by the Dutchman Abraham van Hameln, a successful confectioner and spice merchant. The original house was a beautiful example of classic renaissance architecture completed in 1621. The hand held scales, hanging halfway up on the corner of the house, are a symbol of van Hameln's trade. Today the house is the pièce de résistance of the "New Old Town" project. It has been authentically replicated both inside and out at a cost of €8 million.

> **Top Tip!** It is worth stopping for a drink inside the golden Scales café and viewing the ornate interior. Upstairs, the café connects with the Friedrich Stoltze museum (free entry). Friedrich Stoltze (1816 – 1891) was a Frankfurt poet and writer, known for writing in the local, *Hessisch*, dialect. He was also famed for his pro German unity and democratic stance, often to be read in his own satirical publication, Frankfurter Latern.

The Golden Scales after which the house is named

12. Archaeological Ruins (*Kaiserpfalz*)

Bendergasse 3 - free entry (<u>www.archaeologisches-museum-frankfurt.de</u>)

This exhibit of Roman, and Medieval ruins is open to the public and offers information in both English and German. The ruins were first discovered post WW2 when the rubble of the destroyed houses was being removed. Prior to the New Old Town development, the ruins were part of an open space between the cathedral and Römerberg, upon which the public could sit and children could play. Fortunately today, the ruins are afforded better protection

Frankfurt Cathedral - Kaiserdom

13. The Chicken Market (*Hühnermarkt*)

Formerly this was the old chicken market, but today the reconstructed buildings offer insight into five centuries of architectural styles by standing on the spot and turning 360 degrees: start at the Red House with its typical 14th-century Gothic features, with the upper floors jettying over the lower floors and the steep "pointy" roof. Supported by huge black wooden timbers, the open area was where the butchers would sell their meats and wares. Next door, a similar building progresses into the renaissance period displaying a stone base, instead of timber supports. Next comes the Green Linden House, housing Balthasar wine bar, which is ornately decorated and has a round, ox-eye, window set into the top of the roof typical of a baroque house of the 1700's. On the west side is a row of classicist buildings (numbers 22, 24 and 26) of the nineteenth century; very flat fronted with uniform bands of windows.

Have you spotted the white house, with the plaque dedicated to "Tante Melber"? She was the aunt of the famous German author, Johann Wolfgang Goethe, and as a boy he stayed with his aunt whilst his own family home was being renovated.

The fountain on the square is dedicated to Friedrich Stoltze. He gets a mention in the Top Tip!, on page 41.

14. Hinter dem Lämmchen

Hinter dem Lämmchen 6

Half way along the street called Hinter dem Lämmchen, you will find some large, open, wooden doors leading to typical "Hof", or yard. These Hofs hosted trade fairs during the middle ages. The merchants would lease space on the ground floor to store and trade goods, and rent rooms in the galleried guest houses above. The original Frankfurt Old Town was a series Hofs and inter-connected narrow alleyways

The Friedrich Stoltze Fountain at the Hühnermarkt

15. St. Paul's Church (*Paulskirche*)

Paulsplatz - free entry

Although a church, built in 1790, St Paul's is also the site of the first German parliament in 1848 and, for that reason, the bomb damaged St. Paul's was reconstructed after WW2 as the symbolic "cradle of German democracy". Inside, around the walls on the ground floor, the story of Germany's democratic movement is written in both English and German. The dramatic artwork "The procession of the people's representatives" dominates the centre of the room and is by the renowned Berlin artist, Johannes Grützke. Upstairs the auditorium displays the flags of the 16 states of Germany plus the federal, and city of Frankfurt, flags.

Walking Tour - Hauptwache and Beyond

This walking tour will take you through the shopping area of Frankfurt, up to the Old Opera house and back towards the Old Town via Goethe's house. Two maps for this walk are on the following pages.

16. Indoor Market (*Kleinmarkthalle*)

Hasengasse 5-7

An indoor market hall has stood in Frankfurt since the late 1800's. Rebuilt post war, today's market, with its mezzanine level, offers produce from all over the world but of real interest is the chance to try local dishes such as Grüne Soß (green sauce), Handkäse (hand cheese), Frankfurter sausage and local wines. Schreibers is the famous sausage seller, easily detected by the long queues, whilst many of the other stalls offer small plates of freshly prepared food and places to stand or sit, and enjoy a bite to eat.   Local Rhineland wine is sold by the glass upstairs at the Rollanderhof and you are permitted to bring your own food.

> **Top Tip!** Along the wall, running opposite the north side of the Indoor Market is some local street art. The colourful work depicts aspects of Frankfurt culture from Goethe to green sauce and motifs of Eintracht Frankfurt, the local football team.

17. The Church of our Lady (*Liebfrauenkirche*)

Liebfrauenberg

The Church of our Lady is of a catholic denomination and dates back to the 1300's.

Approach the church from the Liebfrauenstraße, and you will see a mural of a Franciscan monk, underneath which it reads "Welcome to a moment of silence - Capuchin Franciscan Friary" with an arrow pointing left. Follow the arrow to see an opening leading to the peace garden tucked behind the church.

18. The Zeil

The Zeil is the busiest shopping street in Frankfurt. "Zeil" rhymes with "while", so use the ditty, "Shop a while, on the Zeil" to help remember the name! The Zeil has all the big brand stores and on Saturdays is crammed with shoppers and street performers. Remember however, that stores are closed on Sundays, even here on the Zeil.

19. The Bull and the Bear

Börsenplatz

The bull and the bear statues are the international symbols for the rising (bull) and falling (bear) stock markets. They stand outside the German Stock Exchange, (Börse), the large yellow sandstone building, with the flags.

> **Top Tip!** Walk up the steps as if to enter the Börse building and you notice statues of figures representing each of the continents. These statues were originally mounted on the roof of an early Börse building located in the old town. Notice how all are bare foot, except Europa, who has shoes, books and machinery.

20. Freßgass

Große Bockenheimer Straße

Officially this pedestrianised street is called "Große Bockenheimer Straße" but the locals call it the "Freßgass", the eating alley. The nickname originates from medieval times when animals would graze here and uses the German verb to describe animals eating, "fressen". However, today the name Freßgass is a reference to all the cafes and delicatessens located on the street, and is a gentle joke about people having their noses in the trough.

21. The Old Opera House (*Alte Oper*)

Opernplatz

The Old Opera House was originally opened in 1880. However, a bomb dropped through the roof during WW2 and the subsequent fire destroyed the building internally whilst the outer walls remained intact. A lack of city funds meant the Old Opera House stood as a ruin until the late 1970's and finally re-opened in 1981. The concert hall inside is modern, however the first floor restaurant is decorated to look as it would have done in the 1880's.

By the way, the two figures flanking the 1st floor loggia are Goethe to the right and Mozart to the left.

The Bull statue outside the Stock Exchange

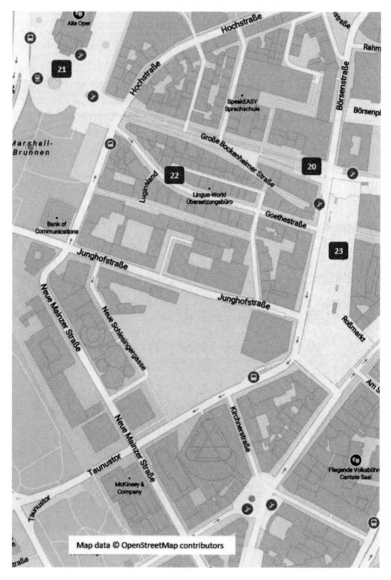

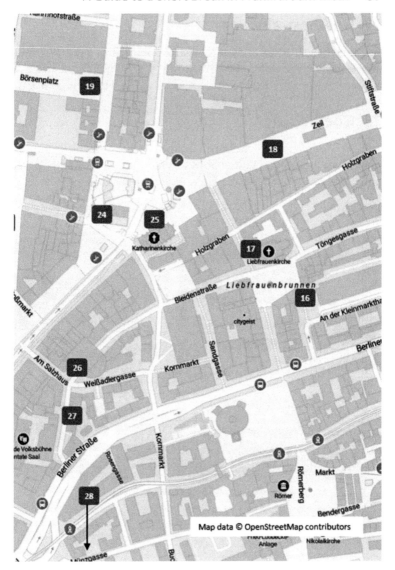

22. Goethestraße

Goethestraße is a street of high-end shops such as Prada, Chanel and Louis Vuitton.   Frankfurt might be a small city but it still has the wealth to support the most famous designer labels in the world.

23. Goetheplatz

Johann Wolfgang Goethe, was Germany's most revered author, playwright and poet. He was born in Frankfurt August 28th 1749, and his place of birth is listed later on during this tour.

Goetheplatz is a good place to observe the rich mix of old and new architecture in Frankfurt. Notice the modern roof of the post office reaching over the old 19th century hotel facade, meanwhile behind other old facades are hidden modern office buildings.

Freßgass' aka Große Bockenheimer Straße

24. The Hauptwache

An der Hauptwache 15

Hauptwache literally means "main watch" and this pretty, ornate, red sandstone building was originally built as a police station in 1729. The area around the Hauptwache was also a place of executions and public punishments. Today the building serves as a café and the name Hauptwache is mainly associated with the underground station that runs beneath it.

25. St. Katherine's church (*St. Katharinenkirche*)

An der Hauptwache 1

Completed in 1681, St. Katherine's was the first church in Frankfurt built specifically for protestant worship. The Goethe family would worship here and famous composers, such as Telemann, Mozart and Mendelssohn have also played here. In those early days the interior was lavishly baroque, however it suffered damage during WW2 and today the decor is far simpler. Within the church, close to the south wall, is a console with a touch screen showing pictures of the old baroque interior.

The Old Opera House - Alte Oper

26. Berlin Wall Art

Am Salzhaus 2

Brought to Frankfurt in 2014 to celebrate the 25th anniversary of the reunification of east and west Berlin, this original piece of the Berlin Wall was painted by the artist Thierry Noir, famed for his art along the wall in Berlin during the 1980's when it was still a divided the city.

27. Goethe House Frankfurter (*Goethe-Haus*)

Großer Hirschgraben 25-27   **www.frankfurter-goethe-haus.de**
Goethe Haus is the birthplace (1749) of Johann Wolfgang Goethe. The original house had to be extensively reconstructed after WW2. Today the house is part of the German Romanticism Museum celebrating romantic art and literature of the period, which includes not just Goethe's works but other manuscripts and illustrations from the romantic and classicist period.

> **Top Tip!** On leaving the Goethe House and heading towards the Carmelite cloister, you will pass the Leica Camera store, Großer Hirschgraben 15, which often has a free photographic exhibition inside on the mezzanine level.

28. The Carmelite Cloister (*Karmeliterkloster*)

Münzgasse 9 - free entry – (**www.stadtgeschichte-ffm.de**)
Founded in the 13th century, today the Carmelite Cloister serves as the city archives. The highlights are the Jörg Ratgeb frescoes in the cloister and refectory, painted between 1514 and 1521. Audio listening devices are available in English if you wish to discover more about the frescoes, and as you wander around the cloister you also have the chance to view Roman artefacts which are over spill from the archaeological museum next door.

Hauptwache and St. Katherine's Church

Additional Short Walks

If you are in Frankfurt for more than 24 hours, it is very easy to explore more of the city by foot. Below are a few more wandering suggestions to explore.

East to the European Central Bank (ECB)

On a sunny day, simply stay on the northern bank (city side) and follow the River Main from the old town, east, towards the European Central Bank. It's a pleasant, relaxing walk, watching the ships and barges coming and going in their unhurried fashion. Early morning the rowers are out and by the afternoon, the Main is dotted with paddle boarders heading east to catch the sunset as they return westwards later on.

Keep going under the next three bridges called the Alte Brücke, Ignatz-Bubis-Brücke and Flößerbrücke and by the time you reach the towering, glass ECB building, you will have stumbled upon the Oosten restaurant, Mayfarthstraße 4, Ostend (https://oosten-frankfurt.com/?lang=en), at the river's edge, with its upstairs sun deck and bar. It's a great place to stop and grab some refreshment, or if you plan ahead, book a table for lunch or dinner. From the restaurant heading further east is a pathway heading north which today serves as a memorial to the Jewish victims of the holocaust who were transported out of Frankfurt from this location. If heading further east along the river bank, under the Deutschherrnbrücke the next location is the Hafenpark, an urban space for ball games, and skate boarders. A little further along, within the arches of the Honsellbrücke bridge, is the Art Gallery - Kunst Verein Familie Montez, Honsellstraße 7, Ostend (https://kvfm.de/innen-malen) which showcases art exhibitions and regularly hosts jazz evenings.

A tram or train back into the city centre isn't far away. Follow Honsellstraße all the way along until you reach Hanauer Landstraße where you will find the Ostbahnhof underground train station, and the tram stop at street level.

The European Central Bank

The Old City Walls - Wallanlagen

The medieval city walls of Frankfurt no longer stand, instead there is a beautiful park, the Wallanlagen, that follows the path of the old walls and makes for an interesting and varied 5km (3.5 mile) walk. Look at any map of Frankfurt and it's easy to spot - it's the ring of green that surrounds the city centre and, at the southern edge, follows the river bank.

There is plenty to see in the park. Ponds and trees provide for birds (keep your eyes open for the resident heron), and there is huge variety of sculptures, of greats such as Beethoven to the lesser known curvaceous Betty.

In the section of the park, at the back of the city centre Hilton hotel is a pretty little garden house, the Nebbiensches Gartenhaus, (www.frankfurter-kuenstlerclub.de) which hosts regular exhibits by local artists. Also close by is the Eschenheimer tower, formerly one of the gate houses dating back to the 1300's, which was the main entry point, from the north, into Frankfurt. Close to the Eschenheimer tower is the café bar, Good Times for Good People, Eschenheimer Tor 3, Innenstadt, which is open from lunchtime and into the late evening and is a good place for a bite to eat and/or drink.

Continue further west around the park towards the Old Opera House and from there the park eventually heads south towards the past the iconic Euro sign, a popular spot for a selfie. Shortly before the Euro sign, tucked into ground floor of one of the modern, tall, office block buildings is Elaine's Deli, Taunus Tor 1-3, Innenstadt. It opens early in the morning for coffee and serves lunch and snacks throughout the day.

The iconic Euro Sign, at the western end of the Wallanlage

The Old Jewish Cemetery and City Model

The old Jewish cemetery is located next door to the Jewish Ghetto museum, *Museum Judengasse*. At the corner of the museum building, on the junction of Kurt-Schumacher-Straße and Battonstraße, look down to see brass plates laid into the ground with house names on them, e.g. Goldenes Schaf. The brass plates outline where some of the ghetto houses previously stood and are part of the museum exhibit. Nothing remains of the ghetto today, however the museum has the foundation stones from some of the original houses, laid out as they would have been in the 15th century, and is the ideal place to visit for more information about life in the ghetto.

The cemetery wall and Neue Börneplatz serve as a holocaust memorial. Embedded into the cemetery walls are small metal blocks listing alphabetically by surname almost 12,000 Frankfurt Jews murdered during the holocaust. Anne Frank was born in Frankfurt and the Frank family fled to Amsterdam to escape the Nazis. Anne's name plate can be found on the north wall.

Commemoration blocks around the walls of the old cemetery

Follow the wall round to the south side towards Neue Börneplatz. On the side of the modern building is a large black, granite, plaque commemorating the site of the Börneplatz synagogue, razed to the ground on November 9th, 1938 during the *Kristallnacht* atrocities. Look down at the ground and a thin metal strip is the outline of where the synagogue previously stood. Neue Börneplatz, formerly the site of the Jewish market place, has today at its centre some of the old foundation stones from the medieval ghetto surrounded by plane trees, each with 6 branches symbolising the six pointed star of David.

The cemetery is kept locked, so if you wish to enter a key can be borrowed from the museum, but only on production of a valid ID card.

Top Tip! The large building housing the Jewish ghetto museum, is also a city municipal building and it houses a "to-scale" model of Frankfurt. Monday to Friday it is free to enter and view. The entrance is on Kurt-Schumacher-Straße 10. On entering walk to the left side of the security desk and through the doors into the atrium housing the city model.

Conclusion

I hope you have a wonderful time in Frankfurt and are charmed, like so many others, at this small city with its beguiling mix of tradition versus modern.

This book is a great start in guiding you to plenty of places to explore and eat, drink and be merry. For more ideas browse the website blog pages at www.walk-frankfurt.com/blog. If you are in Frankfurt during festival time check the following web page for the annually updated dates: https://www.walk-frankfurt.com/monthly-events-in-frankfurt.

For a truly personal experience the best thing to do, of course, is book a guided tour. Have your questions answered, orientate yourself in as little as 90 minutes and discover even more fun facts and information about Frankfurt. All details on how to book a tour can be found on the web page: www.walk-frankfurt.com.

Your Notes

Printed in Great Britain
by Amazon

27501997R00046